Absolute Truth?

Mark Ashton

InterVarsity Press® is the book-publishing division of InterVarsity Christian Fellowship®, a student movement active on campus at hundreds of universities, colleges and schools of nursing in the United States of America, and a member movement of the International Fellowship of Evangelical Students. For information about local and regional activities, write Public Relations Dept., InterVarsity Christian Fellowship, 6400 Schroeder Rd., P.O. Box 7895, Madison, WI 53707-7895.

All Scripture quotations, unless otherwise indicated, are taken from the HOLY BIBLE, NEW INTERNATIONAL VERSION®. NIV®. Copyright ©1973, 1978, 1984 by International Bible Society. Used by permission of Zondervan Publishing House. All rights reserved.

ISBN 0-87784-063-6

Printed in the United States of America ∞

13   12   11   10   9   8   7   6   5   4

05   04   03   02

Have you ever spent fifteen minutes trying to decide what to wear for a date or to a wedding? Have you made a server in a restaurant come back three times while you hesitated about what you wanted for dinner? Have you stood in the video store for thirty minutes or more choosing a movie for the evening's entertainment?

America is a smorgasbord of possibilities. At any given mealtime, you can choose from a vast array of restaurants and fast-food joints. Once inside, a restaurant as simple as McDonald's can provide you with over eighty-five different menu options. Soon we will be able to have more than five hundred cable channels at our fingertips. A college catalog can include thousands of course offerings.

Free to Choose
Even walking down the bread aisle of the grocery store can be an overwhelming experience for the indecisive. A bread shopper is greeted by white, wheat, French, sourdough, Italian, rye, pumpernickel, beefsteak, thick-sliced, thin-sliced, family-sliced, unsliced, Texas-sliced, split-top, buttered-top, dozens of brands, different-sized loaves and prices to fit anyone's budget. The number of choices that we make in a given day, even about mundane things, is phenomenal.

Our consumer society is accustomed to having the choices and selections we want. This mentality has spilled over into the realm of religions, faiths and worldviews as well. Television has brought cultures that were once far away right into our living rooms. Travel has made it possible to see any part of the world within a few days' journey. People once considered foreign both geographically and culturally are now our friends as international students, and multinational corporations have become common. Ideas from around the globe are now accessible to our generation via the Internet. That which used to be thought of as *their* rituals, *their* rites, *their* religions now become *our* options, *our* choices and *our* possibilities.

Pluralism

The smorgasbord of options in our society is better known as *pluralism*. Pluralism is a view that there are many viable options within a society on all levels, especially those of worldviews, faiths and ideologies.

Most would agree that pluralism is a good thing for society. A society that allows people to choose their beliefs is much better than one that imposes a particular faith or ideology on its people, coercing them to subscribe to certain tenets. Life is more enjoyable when one can choose a good movie on a Saturday night, order a hamburger with tomatoes and onions, and be confronted by the thoughts of someone from another culture who believes differently. It is healthy to have assumptions challenged and to look at reality from a different vantage point. The diversity of our society enables us to explore a variety of thoughts and ideologies; this freedom to explore is helpful for minds that want to learn the truth.

Pluralism is good for those who like options, but many people take pluralism one step further by affirming relativistic pluralism, also known as relativism. Relativism affirms the value of many options, but does not distinguish any difference in the validity or truthfulness of these options. Relativism is the view that there are many viable options within a society—at all levels, especially those of worldviews, faith and ideologies—*all of which are equally true.*

Absolute Relativism

Relativism is a very attractive and popular philosophy. On the surface, it appears to be a very charitable, tolerant and livable viewpoint. It treats all human ideologies and moral systems as equal. A true relativist does not have to grapple with moral issues such as premarital sex, copying software or using fake IDs if her personal viewpoint is as valid as any other. She does not judge others for their views, and she expects the same courtesy in return. "Live and let live" is her motto.

When relativism is embraced, one need not get too involved in the affairs of others. Difficult confrontations on such sticky subjects as politics, religion and morality can be easily avoided. Relativists enjoy a comfort barrier between themselves and others because they need only agree that each individual can believe whatever he or she wishes to believe.

Relativism is propagated in university culture all over the United States. Allan Bloom, a University of Chicago philosophy professor, wrote in the opening pages of *The Closing of the American Mind* that "there is one thing a professor can be absolutely certain of: almost every student entering the university believes, or says he believes, that truth is relative."[1]

Recently one Harvard student said in his graduation address, "I believe that there is one idea, one sentiment, which we have all acquired at some point in our Harvard careers—and that, ladies and gentlemen, is, in a word, confusion. They tell us it is heresy to suggest the superiority of some value, fantasy to believe in moral argument, slavery to submit to judgment sounder than your own. The freedom of our day is the freedom to devote ourselves to any values we please, on the mere condition that we do not believe them to be true."[2]

College students who hold that their beliefs are true and that others' beliefs are false are often dismissed as intolerant, closeminded, arrogant or bigoted. Tolerance is valued more highly than truth.

Difficulties with Relativism

If you look around the university to find the most vehement *opposition* to relativism, you will wind up in the philosophy department. Robert Wengert, a philosophy professor at the University of Illinois, often begins his introductory ethics classes by asking how many of the students believe that truth is relative. A show of hands usually reveals that two-thirds to three-fourths of the class thinks in this manner. After discussing the syllabus, testing dates, papers and content of the course, Wengert informs the class that they will be graded according to height. When the smart-alecky tall kid loudly agrees with this system, the professor adds, "Short students get A's; tall students flunk."

Inevitably a student's hand is raised: "Your grading system is not fair."

"I am the professor," retorts Wengert. "I can

grade however I wish."

The student insists, "But what you ought to do is grade us according to how well we learn the material. You should look at our papers and exams to see how well we have assimilated the content of the course and grade us on *that*." The class nods in affirmation (especially the tall students).

Professor Wengert then replies, "By using words like *should* and *ought*, you betray your alleged conviction that truth is relative. If you were a true relativist, you would realize that there is no external standard to which my grading *should* conform. If my truth and my ethic lead me to an alternate grading system that you deem inappropriate, c'est la vie! I will grade however I wish."

After exhorting his class against lazy thinking about relativism and the pursuit of truth, he relieves them by letting them know their grades will actually be based on academic performance.

The first recorded refutation of relativism

goes back over twenty-four centuries. In ancient Greece, a man named Protagoras came up with the theory that "whatever you believe is true." Socrates responded by saying, "Well then, dear Protagoras, I believe that you are wrong!"

Relativism Is Unreasonable

Although there are many reasons why relativism is so strongly denounced among philosophers, I will discuss only two of them. To begin with, relativism is intellectually untenable. Relativism embraces the statement "There is no absolute truth." This proposition refutes itself, because it holds only if the statement itself is absolutely true! It cannot be a true statement, because it asserts its own truth and denies all truth at the same time.

Any class in logic and reasoning will teach the law of noncontradiction as a basic premise. The law of noncontradiction states that *A and not-A cannot be simultaneously true in the same sense.*

For instance, one cannot say "I am in Australia" and "I am not in Australia" and have both statements be simultaneously true in the same sense. Likewise, the two statements "The sun appears in the east in the morning" and "The sun does not appear in the east in the morning" cannot be true at the same time in the same way. The truth is that I am not in Australia and the sun does appear in the east. The way the truth can be determined is by checking the statements against reality. The statement that corresponds with reality is the one that is true and should be believed.

A relativist believes that contradictory terms can be simultaneously true. He might argue, "What I believe is true for me; what you believe is true for you." However, our beliefs do not determine reality. I might believe that I can jump off the Sears Tower and walk on air, while you believe that I will plummet to my death. When I step off the roof of the 104th floor, only you will remain to determine which of us believed what is objectively true. My personal belief in floating will not save me. Belief, even a very sincere belief, does not determine truth.

Relativism Is Unlivable

The second reason that relativism is criticized is that it is unlivable. If there is no absolute truth, then any action that I may take is arbitrary. It makes no difference whether I eat or do not eat. It is no more morally reprehensible that somebody raped your sister than that he shook her hand. Your professor may as well grade on the basis of height. Drinking gasoline is not hazardous to your health. To the true relativist, reason is not reasonable because it is just as likely that the opposite of reason is true.

Further, without absolute truth communication is impossible. Words, sentences and thoughts have meaning only if they have the capacity to express truth. A true relativist might read this booklet and think that I am discussing Chinese rice paddies, because he ascribes his own particular brand of truth to the words that he sees on the page without regard for the intention of the author to communicate meaningful thoughts. Without meaning, communication is a futile exercise of the vocal cords (or pen or computer).

For the student, relativism also makes education an exercise in futility. Why sit through a physics lecture when the formulas are as likely to be false as true? Why read a history text when the words, ideas and events are likely never to have happened and have no meaning even if they did? If there is no truth, the pursuit of truth is a waste of time, money and energy. Derek Bok, former president of Harvard University, put it this way: "Relativism and individualism have rewritten the rules of the game. They have extinguished the motive for education."[3]

If there is no absolute truth, nothing has value. Life is a ridiculous pursuit of meaninglessness. The true relativist, who lives consistently with the belief that there is no absolute truth, seeks to know nothing, does not care for anything, lives for no reason and acts without regard for anyone or anything. Because relativism is both unlivable and unreasonable, it should be rejected by all thinking persons.

Religious Relativism
Certainly there are some areas of life that do belong within the realm of personal opinion. People may legitimately differ on what flavor of ice cream tastes best, what types of clothes they prefer to wear and what pieces of art they think are beautiful. Those who are open-minded should agree to disagree on these matters of taste without serious argument. The things that belong in the realm of opinion and preference give variety and spice to life.

Some would claim that religion belongs in the realm of opinion. Many believe that truth can be absolute—but not religious truth. All religions are thought to be equally valid.

Islam may be preferred over Taoism just as rainbow sherbet may be preferred over rocky road.

Religion is vastly different from ice cream, art and clothing, however, in that it makes truth claims. These claims of truth are made about the reality of our world, the supernatural world, morality, history and life after death. They must be considered carefully when one is determining whether or not to believe a particular religion. The law of non-contradiction applies to the truth claims of religion as strongly as it applies to the truth claims of the physical world.

Consider the following statements:

Either a supernatural being exists—or a supernatural being does not exist.

If this being does exist, either it is an impersonal force—or he/she is a personal being.

Either Muhammad is the seal of the prophets—or he is not.

Either Jesus is the Son of God—or he is not.

Either there is an afterlife—or there is not.

Any one of these statements could be true, but it cannot be true if its contradictory counterpart is true. We should apply the law of noncontradiction in our investigation of world religions and our search for religious truth. Each of the world's religions teaches some truth. There is value to be found in each of them. The pressing question is not "Is there *some truth* in different religions?" but "Are any of them *fundamentally true?*"

Although the world's major religions have some common teachings, especially in the realm of morals, each teaches fundamentally different things about the most important questions of life. Each philosophy, ideology and worldview has commendable aspects in dealing with some of these questions. However, no religion can be completely true if it is wrong about some of life's most important issues.

Questions such as "Where did I come from?" "Is there a God and what is he/she/it like?" "What is the problem with this world?" "What is the meaning of life?" "What will happen when I die?" and "How do I determine what is right and wrong?" top the list of questions for which humans have long sought answers. For a religion to be true, these questions must be answered in a manner that is consistent with reality.

Because each of the world's major religions teaches different, opposing answers to these questions, *no two can be simultaneously true.* Individuals who take their religion seriously must believe that contradictory religions cannot lead them to the goal of their religion. A sincere Zen Buddhist will not believe that you will achieve enlightenment by trusting your life to Jesus. A sincere Jew does not believe that you can please God by worshiping Brahma.

Determining Religious Truth

The most important question that must be asked about these various religions is, Which one is true? That is, Which one best corresponds to the reality of who God is and what he expects of us? Whichever religion *corresponds with reality* is the one with which we should align ourselves.

Although it seems very charitable and open-minded to believe that all religions are equally true, this belief is actually intellectual suicide. The world's religions are essentially too different to believe that any two, let alone all of them, can be ultimately true. Because of this, it is reasonable to seek the one true religion and, once you find it, be willing to trust it to the exclusion of all others.

With such a huge array of religions, where should one start? There are a few basic tests to which one should put any worldview, faith or ideology to determine its truth. First, it should be internally consistent. It should not contradict itself in what it teaches. Second, it should make sense of the world that we experience and answer most of life's pressing questions in a manner that satisfies both heart and mind. Third, it should not be bound by culture, gender, race or economic boundaries. It should appeal to all types of people from all types of backgrounds. Finally, where the religion under consideration directly contradicts other religions, one should appeal to historical evidence and philosophical reasoning to determine which is correct.

I am convinced that Christianity best fits the criteria above. Let me suggest a number of reasons for this decision.

Although the Bible was written by dozens of authors over a span of more than fifteen hundred years, it is amazingly consistent with itself. The Christian worldview is based not on legend but on real history and geography.

Jesus is arguably the most influential person in the history of the world. He has followers from Finland to Fiji, disciples from Detroit to Delhi and believers from Belize to Burundi. People who claim to believe in

Christ cross all barriers of race, gender, age, culture, economics, politics and nationality. Jesus' teachings are better known than those of any other teacher. Philosophy, history and archaeology affirm the truth of Jesus when he is in conflict with other religions.

Another reason to consider Christianity is that it is a historical religion. This makes it much easier to confirm or deny than most others, which are based on a philosophy or set of teachings rather than a person.

If one takes Siddhartha Gautama (the historical Buddha) out of Buddhism, the four noble truths and the eightfold noble path should theoretically still lead you to enlightenment. If one takes the sages who spoke the teachings of Hinduism out of Hinduism, their teachings are still valid and usable. Although Muhammad is the most revered prophet of Islam, Allah could have chosen to use anyone to speak the words of the Qur'an.

Christianity, however, is based not only on the teachings of Jesus but on his very person.

If you take Jesus away, Christianity crumbles. Because he is a historical figure, people can use the historical method to determine his validity.

The Historicity of Jesus

Once you delve into Christianity from a historical perspective, you will find that there are many reasons to trust in its truthfulness. The words of first-century non-Christian writers such as the Jewish historian Josephus and the Roman historian Cornelius Tacitus confirm that Jesus was actually a historical figure who lived, taught and gained a following during the early part of the first century.

Although eyewitnesses claimed that he performed supernatural acts of healing, turned water to wine and raised people from the dead, he was not a mythological figure such as we might find in ancient or tribal cultures. He was a real, live, historical person who ate, slept, had a family and went to parties.

In addition, Josephus and Tacitus confirm that Jesus was a religious leader who was not approved of by the establishment. He was executed by crucifixion during Passover, and his followers believed and taught that he had risen from the dead. His death and resurrection were the focal point of early worship.

Not only are there non-Christian affirmations of much of early Christian history, but at least four authentic eyewitness accounts of the life of Jesus also exist. They were written by some of his earliest followers who listened to him teach, watched him do miracles and traveled with him for three years.

These historical documents are the accounts of Matthew, Mark, Luke and John, called the four Gospels. They are the first four books of the New Testament of the Bible. By any historical measure, these writings are reliable accounts of the life of Jesus. By many standards, they are the most reliable historical accounts of their time. (For a more thorough discussion, read *Is The New Testament Reliable?* by Paul Barnett, IVP.)

Not only does the whole of Christianity rest on the person of Jesus; more specifically, it hinges on one series of events in his life: his death and resurrection. If you take away these events, Christianity falls apart. At least five times during his ministry, Jesus predicted his own death and resurrection. His claims to be God's Son would be validated if he actually did rise from the dead. If not, Christianity would be nothing more than a brilliant but cruel hoax.

The combined accounts of eyewitnesses and other historians give us a clear picture of what happened in the spring of that fateful year, during the three days of Jesus' crucifixion and resurrection.

Jesus was certainly killed on Friday during the Jewish week of Passover, just outside Jerusalem. It was a public execution, performed by expert Roman guards and overseen by a centurion who most likely signed the death certificate. Not only did people watch Jesus die, but in order to be sure of his death, one of the guards thrust a spear into his side and watched blood come out separately from a clear liquid (a sure medical sign of death).

For Jesus' burial, Nicodemus and Joseph of Arimathea (two of his wealthy followers) wrapped him in about a hundred pounds of linens and spices and laid him in a tomb hewn out of solid rock. A very large stone was rolled in front of the tomb, and an entire guard unit was placed in front of the door to prevent grave-robbing.

On Sunday morning, two women came to pay their respects to the deceased and found the tomb to be empty. The guards were in shock, and the disciples did not believe the women until Peter and John checked for themselves. *Nobody ever found the body.*

Jesus then made at least nine separate appearances to different groups of people. Some were his closest friends and family, while others may have only seen him before as a public figure. He appeared to as few as one and as many as five hundred people at the same time.

The ragtag group of uneducated fishermen and tax collectors who were Jesus' disciples began to tell everyone that Jesus had risen from the dead. Within a couple of months, there were over five thousand followers of Jesus in Jerusalem. As people traveled, they told others about Jesus, and within one generation churches were popping up all over the Mediterranean basin—in Europe, Asia and Africa! People believed the eyewitness reports of Jesus' resurrection.

Followers of Jesus were publicly ridiculed, thrown in jail, tortured and even killed. But many of them were so thoroughly convinced of the truth of the resurrection that they would not deny it even to save their own lives. This was not a fantastic story contrived by a conspiracy of brilliant egomaniacs. It was an objective fact that these simple followers of Jesus were convinced of because they had seen him risen from the dead.

Truth and Life

When he was alive, Jesus claimed not only to be the truth but also the life. His resurrection proves that he holds the power over life and death. Once he said, "I am the resurrection and the life. He who believes in me will live, even though he dies" (John 11:25). In his resurrection he made the way for us to have a fresh start with God. He made it possible for us to experience eternity with God in a resurrected body of our own.

Jesus also said, "I have come that they may have life, and have it to the full" (John 10:10). The new life of Jesus is full of forgiveness for personal wrongdoing, knowledge of the truth about who God is and what he desires for us, the hope of spending eternity with him, and the joy of being in a positive relationship with God during our days on earth. The life Jesus offers is far better than anything we could experience without him.

The Truth for You

The historical fact of Jesus' resurrection can become a personal reality for you. Unlike most other religions, Jesus' teaching is that you do not earn God's favor by doing good deeds. You are not accepted because you are basically a good person. Instead, your eternal life has already been "purchased" by Jesus' willing death on the cross.

Because every person in history has done what is wrong in God's sight, we all fall short of his standard of personal holiness. Our wrongdoing separates us from a God who is morally perfect. Without some payment for our evil, we will remain separated from God for all of eternity. Living our way instead of God's way earns us spiritual death.

Fortunately, God knew our dilemma and sent his Son to live a perfect life and to die in our place—his death the payment for *our* sin. He wants us to have eternal life and makes this life possible through Jesus' death on the cross. When we trust in Jesus and his death and resurrection, we enter into a new life with God that will last forever.

It is offered to you as a personal gift from God, the most precious gift imaginable. To be in a positive relationship with God, you must be sorry about and turn from all of your own personal wrongdoing, admit your need for God, believe the historical fact of Jesus' resurrection and allow Jesus to be the leader of your life.

Jesus is the path to eternal life. You must make a decision about him. You can choose to follow him, reject him or remain apathetic. If you choose to reject him or choose to stay uncommitted, you are rejecting all of the love, forgiveness and truth that God offers you.

Jesus' claims to truth were radical and exclusive. In his mind there was room for no alternate path of truth. He is unique among all major religious leaders in his claims about truth. The Hindu sages claimed to *teach the truth.* The Buddha claimed the eightfold noble path would *lead people to truth.* Muhammad claimed that the *truth was revealed* to him from heaven. But Jesus claimed to *be* the truth. He said, "I am the way and the truth and the life. No one comes to the Father except through me" (John 14:6). The locus of truth, according to Jesus, was not merely what he taught, but who he was. He was the embodiment of truth.

Jesus was not tolerant and open-minded about following other religions. He demanded complete and exclusive allegiance of his followers, because he knew all other paths were futile. And still today, the living Christ wants all people to know him and have the incredible life that only he can deliver.

I would like to extend an invitation to you to explore the claims of Jesus further. Talk to God with an honest prayer that goes something like this: "Dear God, I don't know if you're out there, but if you are, will you please show me the truth about who you really are?" Read the firsthand accounts of Jesus' life by Matthew, Mark, Luke and John. Talk with Christians about their experiences in knowing the living God. Look at the historical evidence.

Jesus said, "Ask and it will be given to you; seek and you will find; knock and the door will be opened to you" (Matthew 7:7). If you are honest with yourself and with God, I am convinced that you will arrive at the conclusion that Jesus is the truth—the only truth.

Notes

[1] Allan Bloom, *The Closing of the American Mind* (New York: Simon & Schuster, 1987), p. 25.

[2] Quoted in Robert Bellah et al., *The Good Society* (New York: Alfred A. Knopf, 1991), p. 44.

[3] Quoted in Robert Fryling, "A Campus Portrait," address given at InterVarsity National Staff Conference, January 1992.

Further Reading

Barnett, Paul. *Is the New Testament Reliable?* Downers Grove, Ill.: InterVarsity Press, 1986.

Sire, James W. *Why Should Anyone Believe Anything at All?* Downers Grove, Ill.: InterVarsity Press, 1994.

Stott, John R. W. *Basic Christianity.* Downers Grove, Ill.: InterVarsity Press, 1958, 1971.

Mark Ashton, a graduate of the University of Illinois in marketing and economics, is a campus staff member with InterVarsity Christian Fellowship. In addition to being a popular campus speaker, he is involved in leadership training and development. He lives in Champaign, Illinois, with his wife, Kelle, and son, Caleb.